Love, Luck, and Lore

a guide to superstitions, prayers, spells, and taking chances in the pursuit of love

By Theresa Hoiles and Elizabeth Carr

Illustrations by Robin Campbell

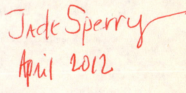

Jade Sperry
April 2012

CONARI PRESS

First published in 2006 by Conari Press,
an imprint of Red Wheel/Weiser, LLC
York Beach, ME
With offices at:
368 Congress Street
Boston, MA 02210
www.redwheelweiser.com

Library of Congress Cataloging-in-Publication Data
Hoiles, Theresa.
  Love, luck, and lore : a guide to superstitions, prayers, spells, and
taking chances in the pursuit of love / by Theresa Hoiles and Elizabeth Carr;
illustrations by Robin Campbell.
     p. cm.
  ISBN 1-57324-204-7 (alk. paper)
  1. Charms. 2. Aphrodisiacs. 3. Incantations. 4. Love. I. Carr,
Elizabeth, 1970- II. Title.
  GR600.H645 2006
  398'.41—dc22

                            2005025561

Typeset in Adobe Minion, Agfa Bliss, and Font Diner by Kathleen Wilson Fivel
Printed in Canada
TCP

13 12 11 10 09 08 07 06
 8 7 6 5 4 3 2 1

Contents

Acknowledgments

Thank you to all the storytellers and matchmakers who have kept mating and dating rituals alive and spirited throughout the centuries. And to all the single girls who have not given up on love. Thank you to our friends who have given us dating advice and a shoulder to cry on over the years. Thank you to those who trusted us with their hearts and sought our guidance; your success in love gave us the confidence to write these pages.

We'd like to thank Dave and Cathy Austin for introducing us to our agent Bill Gladstone. Thank you to Bill for believing in us and dubbing us "datable" enough to sign, Kimberly Valentini for pitching on our behalf, and Conari Press for thinking what we wrote was worth publishing. To Robin Campbell, thanks for the adorable illustrations, we love them. And thanks to Linda Sunshine, Marni Kamins, and Janice MacLeod and Michael Kun for their expert advice. Finally, we would like to thank the companies that folded in order to give us the time to write this book!

Theresa would like to thank . . .

My husband Dave, who is my inspiration; my Mom who has always believed in me; my brothers Nick and Victor and all my family for all their continued encouragement; and, to my friends Rebecca Terlizzi, Michelle Dodge, D'Arcy Nicola, Stephanie Serge, Jennifer Goldberg, Rodney Henson, Jon Gaster, Heidi Rataj, George Putnam, Bernadette McNamara, and the Whittier gang, thank your for all your help and support.

Elizabeth would like to thank . . .

My Mom and Dad who have encouraged my creativity and independence. Thank you to my brothers Ryan and Jonathan, my sister-in-law Jessica, and the rest of my family for always being my rock. Thank you to Kara Delle Donne, Shea Ferlita, and Raven for giving me the tools, the Seinfeld group for their encouragement, and all my girlfriends who keep me laughing and smiling!

Introduction

Welcome, ladies!

Whether you have been a wallflower or are out there dating like crazy, you are certain to learn something new in the pages of this book. We have collected old, new, fun, and odd ways to get out there and find the guy you have been looking for. From simple tasks—such as changing your daily routine (where you buy your morning coffee) or wearing a ring on the first finger of your left hand—to more detailed love spells and dream divinations, these ideas are here to remind you that your heart is open to love.

The key to finding love is to stay positive, open-hearted, and focused on the type of love you want in your life.

There is a saying that when you put something out to the universe, you get it back tenfold.

Here's your chance—take it!

Aphrodisiacs and Spells

The word "spell" evokes visions of pointy black hats and cauldrons, while aphrodisiacs elicit visions of the elusive Venus flytrap. The truth is, aphrodisiacs and spells are some of the most fun, creative, and mysterious ways to find love. Tools to bring love into your life are all around you. Flowers and candles at the corner store, the gems in your jewelry box, and even the salt on your dinner table all have the power to bring you visions of love—it's all in the way you use them. The most important thing is to focus your energy on your efforts; this is the time when the strength of your intentions counts as much as the task at hand. Ask yourself, "Who am I really looking for?"

Enjoy titillating your senses with wonderful concoctions and incantations!

Love Is in Bloom

Lady Montagu was the wife of the British ambassador living in Turkey from 1716 to 1718. She is credited with introducing the sophisticated and subtle "language of flowers" to the Western world. This code began in the harem, as a way of sending covert messages. Below are the flowers associated with love, romance, and courtship. Send a covert message to someone you'd like to get to know better.

Amethyst: Admiration

Carnation, red: Admiration

Carnation, striped: I wish I could be with you

Carnation, white: Sweet and lovely

Chrysanthemum: A heart left to desolation; Truth

Chrysanthemum, red: I love you

Daffodil: Unrequited love or regard

Gardenia: Secret love

Geranium, Rose: I prefer you; Melancholy

Heliotrope: I adore you; Devotion

Honeysuckle: Sweet and secret love

Iris: Wisdom; Hope; Your friendship means so much to me

Ivy: Friendship; Wedded love

Jonquil: Desire; Affection returned

Lilac: New love

Mistletoe: Kiss me

Myrtle: Love; Jewish symbol of marriage

Orange blossom: Marriage and fruitfulness

Peony: Happy marriage; Ostentation; Anger

Red rose: I love you

Rosebud: Confession of love

Tulip, red: Declaration of love

Zinnia, purple: Lasting affection

Potent Potpourri

Use the power of perfume to attract a man by creating a love potpourri. Keep some at home, or take some to work. Try mixing these ingredients:

Fresh rose petals (2 handfuls)
Fresh jasmine petals ($\frac{1}{2}$ handful)
Ylang-ylang oil (3 drops)

Put it all in a plastic bag, shake it up, and pour it into pretty bowls. Decorate your entrance hall, your bedroom, and your desk at work. It is sure to attract compliments and conversation. You could even put some in a cloth pouch and carry it in your pocket or purse to use the aroma to draw a suitor near.

✴ Where to find it ✴

Ylang-ylang oil can be found at your local natural foods store or at various online nutritional supplement sites.

Lover's List

Roses are the universal symbol of love. Try a love spell with roses to find the love of your dreams.

You will need:

1 red rose
1 white rose
1 pink rose
1 candle in any of the three colors
A piece of parchment paper
A red pen
A pink ribbon

Remove all the thorns from the roses and place them in front of the candle. Light the candle. And say:

I call upon the universe,
To hear my call of love.

On the paper, list all the qualities you want in a man. Think hard, don't forget anything, but be careful what you wish for. Wishing for a "hard worker" could bring a workaholic. Once the list is complete, roll the paper around the stems of the flowers. Tie it with the ribbon. And say:

For the greater good, so mote it be.

Luck and Passion

Carnations have a bad rap. They can be beautiful—you just have to get the dyed blue ones out of your head and think about the meanings associated with the colors of carnations: white for pure love and good luck, red for passion. Reintroduce white and red carnations into your life—on your desk at work or at home by your bed. Here's a spell using both powerful colors:

Put one white and nine red carnations in a clear glass vase and fill it with water. Add four drops of red food coloring. Cup your hands around the flowers, take in the smell, and say:

Flowers red I see you,
Touch you,
Smell you.
Bring me love as tangible as you!

Display the flowers so you can see them every day, and be sure to get rid of them as soon as they start to wilt. Dying flowers don't bring luck.

Food Fantasies

Food has played a part in the act of seduction for centuries. Aphrodisiacs in the form of food have been a part of human culture ever since sexual drive began—so much so, that often the first date is over a meal. Some believe that the effects of aphrodisiacs are simply our minds playing tricks on us. But we think these sexy foods have some love powers within. Here is a list of some of the more unusual foods linked to making the heart pound faster. Keep them in mind when ordering a meal on your next date!

Who knew all this sexual power could be found in the crudités platter? Try:

| Asparagus | Radishes | Mushrooms |
| Carrots | Tomatoes | Cucumbers |

Spices that bring natural heat:

| Cinnamon | Garlic | Mint |
| Curry | Ginger | |

Sensual fruit with female implications bring inspiration:

| Artichokes | Mangoes | Peaches |
| Figs | Pomegranates | |

Aroma of Love

In addition to having lots of vitamin A, apricots are known to be a potent aphrodisiac. Try making an apricot love sachet to bring about a lover.

Cut a piece of cloth in a six-inch circle. Place two small dried apricots and a half dozen cloves in the center, and tie it up with a ribbon long enough to wear around your neck. This tantalizing aroma should draw potential lovers your way, leaving men weak in your wake.

Love Stinks

Not only will garlic help ward off vampires, it is also thought to be an herb for protection. And on top of that, it is one of world's great aphrodisiacs. This bulbous clove packs a lot of power.

Poet Percy Bysshe Shelley wrote home during a visit to France, "What do you think? Young women of rank eat—you will never guess what—garlick!"

Put some garlic in your next meal out (and remember to bring breath mints along). See if it attracts a fun-loving guy who wants to protect you too.

Food of the Gods

"Food of the Gods"—you can say that again! That is the loose translation of *Theobroma cacao*, the name of the tree where the cocoa bean grows, the essential ingredient of chocolate. Since 200 BC, people have been enjoying chocolate treats, and they have become a popular gift of love on Valentine's Day as well as other holidays throughout the year. This popularity caused scientists to take a deeper look at chocolate, and it has now been proven to have mood-enhancing qualities. Next time you are in the presence of an attractive man, indulge in a thick, rich slice of chocolate cake. Remember, men love women who indulge every once in a while. Don't be shy!

Sweet Cherries

These sweet, round, juicy red summer berries are a treat any time, and an aphrodisiac that can lure men from miles around. Could there be a more romantic fruit for love?

Here is a cherry trick that can turn a sweet treat into a chance to find out when you are to marry. After eating a bowl of cherries, count the cherry pits, reciting this little ditty: "This year, next year, sometime, never. . . ." Continue until the last pit gives you the answer.

Another way to turn heads with a cherry is to do this fun bar trick. Order a drink with a cherry in it (try a Manhattan, a martini, or—for you nondrinkers—a Shirley Temple). Take the cherry stem and see if you can tie it in a knot while it's in your mouth. This saucy trick is nothing if not a conversation starter.

South of the Equator

Guarana is a berry that grows in Venezuela. Folklore has it that this berry has magical powers. Brazilians have created a very popular soda from the berry, which, like the kola nut, contains caffeine. Its exotic flower and mystical powers are perfect for this Brazilian love spell asking the Ibeji, the twin gods thought to fulfill dreams and desires, to help you find a lover. You will need:

    1 bottle of guarana or any sweet carbonated drink
    1 new pen
    1 piece of clean white paper

Drink half the bottle. With your pen and paper, write a description of the type of guy you are looking for. Write your name and the name of a guy you are interested in, in the form of a cross. If you don't yet know the name of the man you want, use the word "lover" or "husband" instead.

Then ask the Ibeji:

> *I ask you, Ibeji, with all my heart I ask that you come to my assistance and bring me my soul mate soon. Ibeji, I promise you once my soul mate comes to me, I shall give you the other half of this sweet drink.*

Bring your drink and the note to a busy street where people pass by. Put the note under the bottle and leave it there.

✳ Where to find it ✳

Guarana sodas are common in many Latin countries and can be found in markets that specialize in Latin goods.

Gypsy Style

Gypsies are a mysterious traveling tribe, who are thought to hold the key to many magical secrets. The most sought-after secrets are those that involve love. Here is a Gypsy spell to help draw a lover near.

Sit before a fire with a basket of laurel leaves between your knees. Clear your mind of busy thoughts and focus only on your ideal mate. With your left hand, toss a handful of leaves into the fire, and as they burst into flames, recite the following:

Laurel leaves that burn into night's fire,
Send to me my deepest heart's desire.

Repeat three times, and your man will make himself known to you within twenty-four hours.

✷ Where to find it ✷

Laurel leaves are also known as bay leaves and are a common spice. Be warned that they are not for eating, only seasoning.

Light of Love

To conjure a spell to attract a romantic prospect, you will need:

1 red candle
1 white candle
1 pink candle
A vase
Red, white, and pink flowers (choose your favorite)

Arrange the vase of flowers. Light the three candles. Kneel in front of the candles and the arrangement, close your eyes, and say aloud:

I call upon the goddess of love.
I affirm that my heart is open
To the bounty of love you can bring
So deliver quickly
The man of my dreams.
So be it.

Let the candles burn as long as you can, or until they go out naturally.

Harvest of Love

Do a little backyard gardening to find your man.

Try this spell using barley seeds:

Plant some barley seed under an apple tree and chant these words:

Barley, barley, I sow thee
That my true love I might see.
Take thy rake and follow me.

✦ Today's Twist ✦

No apple tree nearby?
After you bury the seeds,
place an apple on top.

Key to Your Heart

Keys are a symbol of luck. Make a key pendulum to predict your future. Tie a key to a string, preferably red, white, or pink. Suspend the key over an empty table, holding your hand still. You can ask any yes or no question about your future love life. If the key swings forward and back the answer to your question is yes. If it sways left to right, sadly the answer is no.

Be Jeweled

Gems and stones carry energy, and, charged with a heart's wishes, they can bring the bearer closer to her dreams. Here is a list of the gems and stones known for their powers to attract love: emerald, garnet, malachite, lapis, moonstone, amethyst, jade, rose quartz (get heart-shaped ones), and of course diamonds.

According to stone magic, the emerald secures love and attracts wealth. Wear an emerald or anything that evokes the power of the emerald, like an emerald-green scarf or sweater, and secure yourself a wealthy man.

The deep red garnet is believed to provide guidance in the night and protection from nightmares. Most importantly, it is the stone of compassion and love. It has been said that women who wear garnet can attract their true love. Go out on the town wearing garnet jewelry or a garnet-colored dress. Let the stone's color guide you toward the love you deserve!

Take two rose quartz stones shaped like hearts and hold one in each hand as you meditate on your true love and what he will bring to your life. Bring the two stones together and bind them with a red string. Place this talisman on your nightstand so it will be the last thing you see before you go to sleep and the first thing you see in the morning. Keeping that love in your mind will help the universe bring him into your life.

Dream On

For centuries, in almost every culture around the world, people have been interpreting dreams. Even if you are a dream-interpreting novice, this dream method can help you locate your true love.

Put a thimbleful of salt under your pillow tonight and you will dream of your future lover. When you wake up tomorrow, write down your dreams and look closely to see where that boy might be hiding!

Yew and You

When the yew tree blossoms, it produces a small berry-like seed. The yew tree is considered sacred and is often found in graveyards and churchyards.

Go to a churchyard you have never visited, and cut a sprig of yew. (Do not eat this plant—it is very poisonous.) Put the sprig under your pillow and you will dream of your future husband.

Tall Drink of Water

Here is an egg superstition that is sure to bring insight into your love life.

After removing the yolk from a hard-boiled egg, heavily sprinkle the white part with salt and eat it before you go to bed. That night your destined husband will bring you a drink of water in your dreams.

Moonlight Prophecy

The moon is responsible for the ebb and flow of the ocean's tides. If the moon can control something that big, how about asking the moon for some help in love? This chant is usually identified with the full moon, but it should also work any time.

Moon, moon, come play your part
And tell me who's my sweetheart,
The color of his hair, the clothes he shall wear,
And on what day he shall appear.

With any luck, tonight you will dream of your future beau.

Gypsy Dreams

Here is a Gypsy trick to dream of your true love. Take a bowl of water and a flat stick. The bowl should be earthenware, and the water should come from a flowing stream (use bottled water if you are not near a stream). A flat stick or piece of wood is laid across the bowl from one edge to the other, forming a bridge. Place the bowl and stick under your bed. As you drift off to sleep, imagine the stick as a small footbridge across an active stream. Imagine yourself crossing the bridge and falling into the stream halfway over—don't worry, someone will rescue you in your dream. The trick is to remember, when you wake up, who rescued you and pulled you from the water. He is the one!

Sweet Dreams

Sweet corn in the summer can bring you sweet dreams. Here's a three-day trick to glimpse a vision of your future husband, using the last of the summer's corn.

Go into a barn at midnight with a colander filled with corn kernels. Leaving the barn doors open, scatter the corn throughout the barn. Do the same thing for the next two nights, and on the third night, you will have a vision of your future husband.

Today's twist

If you don't have access to a barn, try this in a modern location that stores vehicles, such as a garage or shed.

Midnight Fires

This is a spell for you and your girlfriends to do together. On the third day of any month between March and September, an odd number of girls (fewer than nine) string the same number of acorns as there are girls on individual strings. Each girl then attaches her string to a stick and places it in a fire at midnight. They sit in silence until every acorn is burnt. Then, each takes some of the ashes and goes to bed. Repeat this charm:

May love and marriage be the theme
To visit me in this night's dream;
Gentle Venus, be my friend,
The image of my lover send;
Let me see his form and face,
And his occupation trace;
Be it symbol or a sign,
Cupid, forward my design.

It is said that you will all dream about your future husbands.

She-Holly

Here's a holly divination that is sure to tell you who your future lover will be. Gather nine holly leaves with rounded points (the she-holly leaves). Place them in the center of a three-cornered handkerchief or scarf. Tie nine knots in it to secure the leaves, and place it under your pillow before going to sleep. Your future spouse will appear in a dream. It is important that complete silence be observed from the moment you gather the leaves until the moment you wake up the next morning.

✳ Where to find it ✳

Holly branches are abundant around Christmastime at Christmas tree lots and nurseries.

Sow the Seeds of Love

In days gone by, women used hemp seed to help them see their future spouses. Go to a churchyard at midnight, hemp seeds in hand. As you throw them over your left shoulder, recite:

Hemp seed I sow, hemp seed, grow.
He that is to marry me,
Come after me and mow.

A spectral apparition of your future mate will appear with gardening tools in hand, helping you to plant those seeds.

✦ Where to find it ✦

Hemp seeds or hemp seed nuts can be found at natural food stores or through online nutritional sites.

Look Skyward

Too often we wander through life without taking the time to look around at all the wonders in the world. Look up at the sky and see how many shapes you can find in the clouds. Do you see a heart anywhere?

Tonight, if you want to dream of your future husband, go outside and find a star. Stare at it for a long time and then blink three times. Sweet dreams!

Folklore and Superstition

See a penny, pick it up, all day long you'll have good luck! Sayings like this have taken root in cultures near and far. Superstitions are not scientific. They are oral traditions that have been handed down through generations and passed between various cultures. So much so, in fact, that nobody really knows who started "the wrong side of the bed" theory. They may seem goofy and strange, but once you hear them you never forget them, and everyone wants to observe them.

Superstitions are often called "old wives' tales." Hey, if you are looking to be a wife or to find a hot date, why not listen to an experienced wife?

There's Love in Clover

A clover's first leaf is for hope, the second is for faith, the third is for love, and the fourth is for luck! In 1620, Sir John Melton wrote: "If a man walking in the fields find any four leaved grass, he shall in a small while after find some good thing." Put the four-leaf clover you find to good use to find love.

This perfect little leaf is a rare occurrence in nature, but florists today seem to have found a trick and made it more readily available. Try a few tricks of your own:

- Place a four-leaf clover beneath each of the four corners of your bed sheets and you will dream of your future husband.
- Hang a four-leaf clover over the doorway and the first single man to enter will be yours.
- Put it in your shoe at the beginning of the day, and you will see your future husband in a dream that night. But if you wear a *two-leaf* clover in your right shoe, the first man you meet will either be your husband or have the same name as the man you are to marry. This rhyme says it all!

> A clover,
> A clover of two,
> Put it in your right shoe;
> The first young man you meet,
> In field, street, or lane,
> You'll have him or one of his name.

Luck of the Irish

The Irish culture is steeped in folklore about fairies, banshees, and leprechauns. Considering Ireland's strong contrasting Christian beliefs, it is amazing that the two worlds coexist. Here is an Irish superstition that brings the two together:

Put a four-leaf clover in a Bible and carry it around. The next single man you meet while holding it will be your future lover. You might want to find a pocket Bible so he doesn't mistake you for a nun!

An Apple a Day, a Boyfriend Will Stay

Here are some apple tricks to help you find your man:

Press the seeds of an apple against your forehead. The number of seeds that fall off tells you the number of days it will be before you meet your beau.

Wet three apple seeds, give each a man's name, and shoot them through a straw toward the ceiling. The seed that sticks to the ceiling reveals the name of the person who loves you.

Think of the names of five or six men you might want to date. Twist the stem of the apple and say the names in order, until the stem falls off. The last name you say when the stem falls off is the name of the man you will marry. Hard-pressed for names? This also works with the alphabet, to find his first initial.

The Cuckoo

Tradition says when you hear a cuckoo for the first time in the New Year, you should say:

Cuckoo, cuckoo, answer truly, you'll tell me in how many years I'll married be.

The number of times the cuckoo replies is the number of years that will pass before you marry.

Try again in springtime. In Norway, it is believed that if the cuckoo's first call in spring comes from the east, anyone who hears it will be lucky in love.

Snail Mail

Is he coming to you at a snail's pace? Find a snail and try this:

Put a live snail in a glass fruit jar covering the top with cheesecloth and securing it with a rubberband. Leave it there overnight. In the morning, the initials of the man you are to marry will be outlined on the inside of the jar by the snail's slimy track.

Love, Luck, and Lore

Ladybug

In Sweden it is believed that when a ladybug lands on a woman's hand, it is measuring her for a wedding glove. Next time you see a ladybug, carefully capture it and speak the following rhyme:

Fly away east, fly away west,
Show me where lives the one I love best.

Release the ladybug into the air, and the direction it flies will show you where your future lover lives. Some believe that this is the rhyme to say:

Lady, lady lanners,
Take your cloak about your head
And fly away to Flanders.
Fly over moor and fly over mead
Fly over living, fly over dead
Fly ye east or fly ye west
Fly to him that loves me best.

Spice It Up

Using salt and pepper, you can find out if your love is true. Put a spoonful of pepper and a spoonful of salt on a cold cookie sheet sitting on the stovetop. Turn on the burner to light a fire. If the salt and pepper begin to burn, your true love loves you back.

Fire and Water

This may remind you of a third-grade science fair, but it's a surefire way to predict love. Fill a saucer with water. Hold a glass upside down, strike a match and put it under the glass, count to three, and immediately place the glass on top of the saucer. If the water is sucked up into the glass, it's a sign you have a sweetheart who loves you.

Plum Good

Plums are a delicious fruit that also carries the power of prophecy. Here is an old superstition that will let you know if the one you care for loves you back.

Take the pit of a plum and throw it into a fire. Recite the following:

If he loves me, crack and fly;
If he hates me, burn and die.

Say the man's name. If he loves you, the pit will crack and fly out of the fire. If not, it will burn to ash.

Nutty Trick

Nuts are often used in fortunetelling. This trick requires two hazelnuts. Name one hazelnut after yourself and the other after a potential lover. Put them together in a fire. If the nuts burn together, your love is meant to last. If they fail to burn or fly apart, your love is not meant to be.

Love at First Sight

Some believe that where you meet a lover is just as important as when you meet one.

If at all possible, you should meet a lover on a hillside near heather. If you can, meet near a stream, river, or the seashore. If water isn't your thing, meet in the heart of the woods. If that's not practical, who says you can't have that first-date coffee near a body of water or a cluster of trees? Follow these rules and you will have a loving relationship forevermore.

New Moon

On the first night of the new moon, go outside and sit on a rock. Place your bare feet on the rock and lean back against a tree. Look at the moon without blinking and repeat the following:

All hail to the moon, all hail to thee!
I pray thee, good moon, reveal to me
This night to whom I'll wedded be.

Then, it is said, during the night you will dream of your future husband.

Full Moon Fantasy

A full moon tends to have great power. It can make people do crazy things, and some believe it can also bring good fortune. A full moon should also be looked at as a way to find love. Here is a way to find out who your true love is, on the night of a full moon.

Bake a cake when the moon is full. The person who eats the first piece of cake, other than family members, will be your true love.

Evening Stroll

Enjoy a lovely stroll this evening and try out this old English custom.

Go with a girlfriend into the park after dark, hold the tip of a leaf, and recite the following:

If I am to marry near,
Let me hear a bird cry.
If I am to marry far,
Let me hear a cow low.
If I am to single die,
Let me hear a knocking by.

Fairies of Fortune

Dryads are fairies who live in trees in the woods. If you live near an oak, ash, or thorn tree, leave a gift of sweet bread. If you find a leaf on the ground, carry it around and it will bring you good luck. Do not pick the leaf from the tree or it will have the opposite effect.

The hamadryads are female nature spirits who live in oak trees. Wear an oak leaf in your hair to honor these spirits. According to folklore, if you kiss an oak tree, or offer a gift to the tree nymphs who live there, they will send you a blessing in return. Pucker up and hope the next thing you kiss is a man.

Ash Leaf

Here is an ash tree superstition from Northumberland that is sure to find you a mate.

Look for an even ash leaf and recite the following as you pull it from the tree:

> *Even, even ash,*
> *I pluck thee off the tree.*
> *The first young man that I do meet,*
> *My lover he shall be.*

Then put the leaf in your left shoe, and the first single man you meet thereafter will be your love.

✳ Where to find it ✳

Ash leaves can be found at your local tree nursery. An ash leaf is considered "even" when the number of leaflets is the same on each side of the stem.

Branching Out

Gather a piece of oak with an acorn attached to it. Add a piece of ash tree with some seeds. Keep these under your pillow for three consecutive nights. Say the following each night and a man will soon be in your sight:

Acorn cup and ashen key,
Bid my true love to come to me;
Between moonlight and firelight,
Bring him over the hills tonight;
Over the meadows, over the moor,
Over the rivers, over the sea,
Over the threshold and in at the door,
Acorn cup and ashen key bring my true love to me.

Flowers and Branches

In Norfolk, girls went out early on May mornings and gathered bunches of red or white hawthorne flowers. Returning home in silence, they would then decorate the house with them. If a girl spoke to anyone on the way, it was believed she was sure not to marry that year. But if she maintained her silence, love was sure to come her way.

Another way to find love with the help of a hawthorne tree is to hang a flowering hawthorne branch on a signpost at a four-lane crossing. The next morning, see which way the wind has blown it. That is the direction from which your man will come.

Sage Leaves

Sage is a favorite herb of the Hungarian Gypsies. Hungarian folklore says that a single woman should go into a garden (a backyard will suffice) at midnight and pick twelve sage leaves. If she holds them to her heart, a shadowy form of her future husband will approach. Brave the night and see what it brings.

It's a Ring Thing!

The rings you wear on your fingers often give others a sense of who you are. But there is also a language of rings that gives meaning to the placement of a ring on each finger. What message do *you* want to send?

Ring on the first finger of the left hand: I want to be married.

Ring on the second finger of the left hand: I prefer platonic friendship.

Ring on the third finger of the left hand: I am engaged or married.

Ring on the fourth, or little, finger of the left hand: I never intend to marry.

Turning to Love

The wedding ring—a perfect circle with no beginning and no end. The wedding ring became a common custom in Roman times and was worn on the ring finger of the left hand. The Romans believed that this finger had a special vein, *vena amoris*, or "the vein of love," that ran directly to the heart. Today, the ring means: "Off limits, I'm taken."

Use the help of your married friends to find love. Hold a married person's left hand in yours, and rotate the ring on his or her finger three times. Repeat this on the hands of fourteen people. When the spell is complete, you will see your future love. Introduce yourself!

Here's another ring superstition that is sure to tell you who will be buying you a ring someday. Pass a piece of cheese through a wedding ring three times. Then lay the ring under your pillow. You will dream of your future lover that night.

Wedding Ring Pendulum

Here is a game you can try using a gold wedding ring and a hair from your head. Thread the hair through the ring, and hold the ends of the hair between the thumb and forefinger of your left hand. Place your elbow on the table and gently lower the ring into a glass, suspending it until it is centered. Hold your arm still. If the ring doesn't move at all, it will be a long time before you marry. If it moves from side to side, hitting the glass, count the number of times it hits in a five-minute period. Subtract that number from the number of letters in your first and last names. That is the number of years before you are to be married. If the number is a negative number, you will be married within the year.

Sweet Pea

Using peas, try this method to find out when you will marry.

Put a pea pod with nine peas over the door. If a married man comes under it first, you will not be married within the year. If a single man does, you will be married within the year.

That pea pod can tell you more! Unmarried women used to search for a pea pod containing nine peas and put it on the floor near their front door with a note that read, "Come on in, my dear, and do not fear." The first single guy to come in through the door was the woman's true love.

Let Them Eat Pie!

Invite your single girlfriends over for afternoon tea, and of course a slice of fresh-baked pie. The secret is to first hide a ring inside the pie. Whoever finds the ring in her slice of pie will be the next one to get married.

Remember to eat the first bite of a pie from the side. Legend has it that a woman who eats the point first will never get married.

Turkey Bones

Ozark women believe that carrying turkey bones or the gobbler (the neck) concealed in your clothing makes a great love charm. That may sound pretty gross to us, but if something works, it can't hurt to try it.

Blooming Onions

They may be smelly and make you cry, but onions have a secret power. Name four onions and put them under your bed. The onion that sprouts during the night has the name of the man who loves you.

✦ Today's twist ✦

You might want to seal the onions in a plastic bag to contain the aroma.

Half Nuts

Some French countrymen may still believe in the sensual powers of the walnut tree. In order to gain affection from a lady, they would secretly place a leaf from a walnut tree in lady's shoe. Here's something for you to do about that male friend in your life who you think can be more. Divide a walnut or hazelnut with the one you admire; if he accepts the half you offer, and is silent while you both share this aphrodisiac, your love will be returned.

Recipe for Love

In northern England, young maidens would use this formula to meet their knights. Bake a cake (use any recipe for a cake) in silence. Place it on the hearth (a stove will suffice) and carve your initials in the top of the cake. Leave the door to that room open, and your future spouse or his spirit will come in and carve his initials next to yours.

Fishy Sticks

Here is a great herring divination to get some info on your future love.

To know if he will be attractive and trustworthy:

Throw the white membrane of the herring at the wall. Look at the way it sticks to the wall. If it is straight, he will be good-looking and very trustworthy. If it doesn't stick or is crooked, he's gonna be a loser. (Take a few practice shots first!)

Mint Sprig

We just love those Irish love superstitions. To cause love, keep a
sprig of mint in your hand until the herb grows moist and warm.
Then take hold of the hand of the person you love, and he will
follow you as long as your two hands close over the herb. No
invocation is necessary, but silence must be kept between the two
parties for ten minutes to give the charm time to work.

Milky Way

Milk may do a body good, but it will also make your love wishes come true. Have a glass of milk. Make a wish as you pour the milk into your glass. Put the milk container back in the refrigerator and put a coin under it. At the end of the day, give the coin to a person in need so that the magic of giving energizes your wish.

The Snowdrop

The snowdrop is said to bring hope. The Danes used to press this delicate flower and present it to their sweeties on Valentine's Day.

Wear one and show you have hope that there is a man out there for you. Maybe the flower's sweet perfume will draw him closer. At the end of the day, press the flower so you will have it to give to your true love when he arrives.

Flowers in the Air

Cowslip is a spring flower associated with divination. Make a ball of cowslip flowers. A fun prophecy is to say to the ball, "Tissy-tossy, tell me true, who shall I be married to?" Throw the ball in the air while saying various guys' names. When the ball lands or comes apart on the name being said, that is the name of the man you are to marry.

✷ Where to find it ✷

Cowslip flowers can be found at your local florist.

Holly Leaves

You can predict your marital future by counting the number of prickles on a holly leaf and reciting, "Girl, wife, widow, nun." The name you land on with the last prickle is your destiny.

Rose-Colored Dreams

Pluck a full-blown red rose during the month of June by seven o'clock in the morning and put it in a white envelope. Seal it with wax and mark it with your left-hand ring finger. Put the envelope under your pillow and remember your dreams that night.

You will be married within a year if your dreams are of water, fields, flowers, mountains, glass, children, parents, organ music, silver, or the moon. If you see giants, animals, birds, fish, paper, a looking glass, or the sun in your dreams, that means you will be married in five years.

Sweet Nothings

Gypsies have often asked donkeys and mules about love. Find the mule with the longest ears. Whisper in his ear, "Will I fall in love soon?" If the answer is yes, the mule will shake its head. If the mule moves one ear, maybe you will marry soon; if its ears don't move, you will have to wait a while.

Here's a tip: State your question in a breathy voice—the donkey or mule is sure to shake his head!

Love, Luck, and Lore

A Game of Hearts

Magicians' card tricks have astonished people throughout the years, and some believe there is a bit of magic associated with finding love. Card reading has been a fun way of finding out one's future for many centuries. Here is a game that involves regular playing cards. To find who among a company of women will be the first to marry, deal a round of playing cards face upwards. The lucky gal who gets the king of hearts will be the first to find love.

Red Hot for Love

Red cars statistically get more speeding tickets. That's because red grabs attention and makes the heart beat faster.

The Gypsies believe red is a color for love. If you find anything red, pick it up. Say the following: "Red is my blood, and red is my heart. Lucky in love; never keep us apart."

Leafy Lesson

There are many ways to find true love, but who would have thought that you could find out about love over lunch? Well, not exactly over lunch—more like *in* your lunch.

Make a salad. Add some great aphrodisiac veggies to it like artichokes, carrots, cucumbers, and tomatoes. The number of leaves that fall from the bowl indicates the number of years it will be before you marry. Toss carefully.

The Naked Truth

Use this Ozark tradition to find love:

Wet your nightgown and hang it in front of the fireplace or heat vent to dry. Go to bed wearing nothing but your birthday suit. As legend has it, your future mate will enter the room just as one side of the nightgown is dry and rotate it for you before leaving the room. Remember that vision, that's who you are looking for.

Love Scrub

An old Gaelic saying goes, "Rub thy face with violets and goat's milk, and there is not a prince in the world who will not follow thee." Which countries still have princes?

Three Nights 'til Love

Select three things you wish to know about your love; write them down with a new pen in red ink on a clean sheet of paper. Cut off all the corners and burn them. Fold the paper into a true lover's knot and wrap three hairs from your head around it. Place the paper under your pillow for three successive nights.

Dreams over these three nights will tell you who your man is, when you will meet him, and when you will marry.

✦ Where to find it ✦

There are several versions of the lover's knot.
Go online to find your favorite.

To a T

Place your shoes on the floor so that they make the letter T. Then repeat out loud:

Hoping this night my true love to see,
I place my shoes in the shape of a T.

That night you'll dream of your true love. Make all those shoes in your closet work for you.

Start Anew

We all have a guy or two who sticks in our heads and hearts. You have to let go of the past to move on to the future, so use this old superstition to rid yourself of any excess baggage.

Boiling a dishcloth while thinking of those bad boys is believed to chase them away. Just as a hot shower washes away the dirt of the day, this will help you wash your love wounds away—at the very least you'll have a sterile dishcloth.

At Your Fingertips

Name the four fingers on your left hand for each guy in your life who tugs at your heartstrings. Squeeze your left hand tightly with your right hand. Whichever finger hurts the most has the name of the man you should be with.

Cuts Like a Knife

To find out if your love will have light or dark hair, put a table knife with a white handle on a table. Spin it around. When the knife stops spinning, if the blade faces you, your love will have dark hair. If the handle faces you, he will be light-haired.

Love Is Blind

In Scotland, young women used "the trial of three dishes" to get a glimpse of their future husbands. Women led other single women blindfolded into a room containing three dishes—one empty, the second filled with clean water, and the third filled with dirty water.

If the blindfolded person placed her hand in the clean water, she would marry a bachelor. If the hand was placed in the dirty water, she would marry a widower. But if she put her hand in the empty dish, she would never marry. The trial should be repeated three times, rearranging the dishes each time.

A Horse Tale

According to English superstition, the colors of horses can help you in finding love. Here are a couple of horse superstitions to try:

Each time you see a gray horse, make a wish. After counting twenty gray horses, you will meet someone with red hair. After that, the next man you meet will be your great love.

Count ten white horses. You will marry the first single man you see upon completing your count.

✦ Today's Twist ✦

Don't live in horse country? Count those steel horses or something with a lot of horsepower.

Bunny Hop

What animal gets more grief for its overactive mating habits?
Why not, when the mating dance is leaping, cavorting, dancing,
and frolicking about? Perhaps this ritual will bring you closer to
a mating dance of your own. It is lucky to say "Hares, hares" as
loud as you can before you go to bed, and to say "Rabbits, rabbits"
as soon as you wake in the morning.

Gods and Goddesses

People have always sought the guidance of a higher power. In most forms of worship, each deity has a special talent. When it comes to love, gods and goddesses play out a celestial soap opera with love lost, found, and unrequited. Learn how to find the beauty of Aphrodite in you, feel the strength of Durga and the tranquility of Rada. Flirt with these ethereal creatures and see what their power and attention brings your way.

Sacred Flame

Vesta was depicted by the ancient Romans as a beautiful woman who held a torch and a votive bowl. She was a popular household guardian. Ever heard of the vestal virgins? These were the mortal attendants who were selected to guard Vesta's sacred flame.

Try this love spell with a candle, and ask Vesta for some guidance.

Place two white candles on either side of a pink candle, with about six inches between them. Light all three candles and recite the following prayer:

Goddess Vesta, please,
Help me to see
The man who will light
The fire of love
Within me.

Move the two white candles (you and your future love) an inch closer to the central pink (love) candle. Do this hourly until the candles are almost touching. Let the candles burn out, and wait for love to arrive.

The Huntress

Diana is the Roman goddess of the hunt, and this book is about hunting for a man, so try this little meditation as you ask Diana to help you with your hunt.

Diana, goddess of the bow,
Patroness of the hunt,
Guide my head and heart
And empower me as the Huntress of Love!

Love and Romance

Hera is to the Greeks what Juno is to the Romans, the goddess of love and marriage. She is the most beautiful of the immortals. Her beauty is even greater than Aphrodite's. Each spring her beauty (and virginity) is renewed when she bathes. Celebrate the goddess of love, romance, and humor by invoking her powers:

In my soul there is a flame
Calling out for the love of another.
Help him hear my call
Bring to me my heart's desire
Guide me toward my destiny
For it is true love I seek.
Oh Hera, hear my prayer!

Empowered Petals

Aphrodite is the Greek goddess of love, beauty, and sexual rapture. She was loved and adored by both men and gods, and many looked to her to find love and sexual desire.

Dress in white and go outside, making sure you have a clear view of the sky. Carry a box of rose petals (a symbol of Aphrodite) and a wand. Look up to the sky and recite the following as you charge the rose petals with Aphrodite's power of love:

Hear me, Aphrodite, goddess of love,
Let your magic empower these rose petals
To draw in my true love.
The spell has been cast, so be it.

Take the rose petals and spread a few around your home, and quietly drop a few at the next party you go to. Talk and flirt up a storm.

Wheel of Fortune

Fortuna is the Roman goddess of good fortune and happiness. She is often depicted standing on the wheel of fate and mostly appealed to women seeking prophecy.

If she liked you, she would shower you with good luck. If she didn't like you, you would have no luck at all.

Try to get on her good side and ask politely if she would send some luck your way in the love department.

Love and War

Durga, the Hindu warrior goddess, is called upon for protection of all that is sacred. Ask Durga to protect you as you continue your search for love.

Today, light a yellow candle and say:

Durga, the goddess who protects all that is sacred,
Take care and watch over me,
Guide my choices with truth, and guard against
Those whose intentions be not true.
In your name, Durga, so be it.

Shake It Up

Holle is a Northern European triple goddess, the Maiden, the Mother, and the Crone; she embodies the three stages of womanhood. In one form, she is seen as a woman from the front and a tree form the back.

Find an elder tree and shake it, as you say:

Sweet Elder, I shake, I shake.
Tell me, ye dogs that wake,
Where is my lover tonight?

Listen closely—the goddess Holle will send her white dogs barking in the direction of your true love.

Moonlit Serenade

Selene is the Greek moon goddess. She was known to have had a countless list of love affairs. This long list includes Zeus, Pan, and her most prolific love with the shepherd Endymion, whom she seduced while he was sleeping in a cave. Together they had fifty daughters. Selene had a deep love for him, and she begged Zeus to let her lover determine his fate. Endymion asked to never grow old and to sleep eternally. Selene visited her dreamy lover every night and kissed him with her rays of light.

It is said that a moonlit night brings the feeling of romance. On a full-moon night, when Selene's power is at its height, don her colors of white and silver. Ask her to shine her rays down on you and empower you with her beauty, grace, and insatiable appetite for love.

Burning

Volcanalia is a festival to the god of fire and the forge, Volcanus. The Romans lit bonfires to honor him, and great feasts were held.

To honor him and ask his favors for your love life, take these two steps: First, to clear the air, burn a bundle of sage and walk throughout your house carrying it. Let the smoke float into all corners of your home, burning away the negative energies. Step two, burn an incense of love. Try rose or jasmine. Ask Volcanus to bring you a man with burning love in his heart.

Visions

Hathor is the Egyptian goddess of love, beauty, and cows. Try this divination as you invoke the beauty within you and Hathor's powers.

Sit alone in front of a mirror, drinking a glass of milk and brushing your hair. Think about the beautiful goddess Hathor and envision yourself the same way. As you do this, you will soon see a vision of your future husband in the depths of the mirror.

Heartfelt Thoughts

Honor the woman who stole Krishna's heart. The Hindu deities Radha and Krishna experienced a divine love and rule the celestial skies together.

To look for your divine lover, light some incense (try patchouli), sit in the lotus position, and meditate. Think about your divine love. As the incense rises and fills the room, ask Radha to guide you toward an eternal love.

Sexy Lily

The Greeks started the legends regarding the lily flower. White lilies were created from the milk of the goddess Hera. She had a little help with this flower; Aphrodite put the phallus-like part of the flower, called the pistil, in the center of the lily. Call upon both Aphrodite and Hera to bring you love. Place a vase of lilies in your window or on your desk at work. Ask that they bring men from near and far to your heart and home.

Body Polish

In Greek mythology, Aphrodite was born of the sea foam, and from the foam the sea carried this beautiful goddess to the island of Cyprus. Having been born from the ocean, Aphrodite is associated with salt and salt-water baths. Make an appointment at your local spa and have an Aphrodite-like salt scrub. If a spa is not in your budget, treat yourself to a home salt scrub. Polish your body and gain the Aphrodite glow that no man can resist.

Aphrodite had many lovers, both mortal and immortal. So you shouldn't be shy when asking for a great love. Try this rite to call upon Aphrodite's seductive powers.

The Mother Goddess

The Welsh mother goddess, Cerrdwin, had a cauldron of a never-ending liquid that provided creativity, knowledge, and inspiration. Her celebration comes at the halfway point in the year, to encourage persistence. Call upon Cerrdwin to inspire you in your search for love. Use these love herbs to clear your soul and cleanse body and mind. Create a cauldron using a large mixing bowl. Boil some water and pour it into the bowl. Add chamomile, peppermint, and lemon zest. Drape a large towel over your head to your shoulders. Lean over the bowl, breathe in the aroma, and concentrate on your love desires.

✶ Today's twist ✶

This is also a great way to open your pores and ready your skin for a facial. Why not take advantage of the herbs' powers and pamper yourself with one?

Private Parts

Sheelah is the Irish goddess of fertility and sexuality. She is an Earth mother who is worshipped by the Irish Celts. She is portrayed as a nude female figure with abundant breasts, squatting and holding her private parts wide open. Her image was supposed to promote fertility and romance. Buy a Sheelah amulet and wear it, if you dare. If anything, this will certainly make a great conversation piece.

Fruit of the Vine

Dionysus is the Greek god of wine and fertility. He is said to have brought in the heat that rid the world of winter and gave the promise of summer. Where is a better place to celebrate Dionysus than your local wine cellar? Sign up for a wine-tasting class or wine tour. Share a glass with a stranger.

The Protectress

The Egyptian goddess Isis is seen as a protectress. She was the wife of Osiris, whom she desperately mourned when her brother, Seth, slew him and dropped his body into the Nile. Because of her devotion to Osiris, she is known as the goddess of love. Together with her powers of magic, she helps guide many in love, answers faithfulness divinations, and influences destiny. A stone associated with her is amethyst, a well-known love amulet. Wear an amethyst and go look for your destiny.

Saintly Folk

Saints: Are they real or fiction? Can stories of martyred virgins and miraculous streams really be true?

Whatever the case is, these folks are honored for their selfless acts on earth, and many gave their lives for their true love of and devotion to God. Throughout the centuries, people have found many ways to honor them and ask for their help and guidance on their own path in life. Here are some saints who are particularly good at helping in the love department. Prepare for wacky dream divinations, have fun with eggs, and practice your apple peeling. Find out what saints and penis-shaped cakes have in common. Most of the rituals can be performed any day of the year, but they might work best on the saint's chosen day.

St. Basil (January 1)

St. Basil was one of the forefathers of the Greek Orthodox Church. He was known for his kindness and charity to the poor. Many celebrations are held in his honor, including this ritual for love.

Place a branch of sweet basil and a branch of an apple tree in a vase with water. Leave them there until morning, and you will dream of your future husband.

St. Basil's day is January first, so if you are thinking about starting the New Year out right, do this trick and envision what you should be looking for all year long!

✦ Where to find it ✦

Basil is readily available yearround in the fresh herb section of most supermarkets or produce stores. A bunch of loose leaves can substitute for a branch.

St. Mark (April 25)

Legend says that on this night women can dream of their future husbands if, before going to bed, they eat a hard-boiled dove's egg sprinkled with salt. For added strength, place a tulip (St. Mark's flower) in a vase by your bed.

If you have trouble finding a dove's egg, here's another way to call upon St. Mark's help: If you're an unmarried woman, leave a flower on the porch and return at midnight. You will see a ghostly apparition of your future husband.

St. Agnes (January 21)

It is said that Agnes's beauty is what got her in so much hot water. She had many suitors, but chose God. In fact, she chose to be martyred rather than married. She may never have found her love in the flesh, but she may have a few connections.

It has also been said that by calling upon St. Agnes and doing the following, you will have visions of your future husband. Fast for twenty-four hours and then eat a salted egg just at bedtime. You will meet your future husband in your dreams that night.

Recite this prayer to Agnes, to dream of your love:

Fair St. Agnes, play thy part
And send to me my own sweetheart
Not in his best or worst array
But in the clothes he wears each day,
That tomorrow I may him ken
From among all other men.

St. Lawrence (August 10)

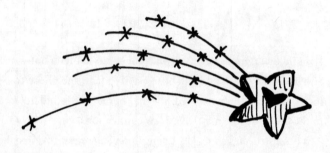

The feast day of St. Lawrence occurs around the same time as the Perseid meteor showers, and the Italians sometimes refer to this as "The Tears of St. Lawrence." They also believe that if you go outside on the night of St. Lawrence's Day, you should look to the sky for answers. If you see a falling star, you will dream of your future husband.

St. Faith (October 6)

St. Faith was another virgin martyr, but in northern England, women would bake St. Faith's cakes in hopes of seeing a divination of their future husbands.

With three girlfriends, make a cake of flour, sugar, salt, and water. Turn the cake nine times as it is baking. When it is done, divide it among yourselves. Divide each portion into nine portions and pass each piece through the wedding ring of a married woman seven times. Next, eat each portion while saying the following:

> *O good St. Faith, be kind tonight*
> *And bring to me my heart's delight.*
> *Let me my future husband view*
> *And be my vision chaste and true.*

When this is complete, go to bed without speaking. You will dream of your future husband tonight!

St. Luke (October 18)

St. Luke was believed to give girls some insight into their future husbands. To invoke his assistance, create a paste of flowers, spices, and vinegar. Spread it on your breasts and lips before going to bed, and repeat three times:

> *St. Luke, St. Luke, be kind to me,*
> *In dreams let me my true love see.*

It is said that a smiling man in your dream is to be a true husband; a rude guy will stray whenever he gets a chance.

St. Andrew (November 30)

St. Andrew is the patron saint of Scotland. Many women have prayed on the eve of St. Andrew's Day in hopes of finding the man of their dreams. You must fast all day, put any man's clothing under your pillow, and pray to St. Andrew before going to bed. That night, you will dream about your future husband.

Another method associated with St. Andrew that gives you fifty-fifty odds is the following:

Throw a shoe at a door. If the shoe lands with the toe pointed in the direction of the exit, then tradition says that you will leave your parents' house and marry within a year.

St. Lucy (December 13)

St. Lucy is the patron saint of virgins. The name Lucy means "light." Her day is celebrated in Norway and Sweden, where she is known as the "queen of light."

Let her bring light your way—or at least a vision of your future husband. It is believed that if a woman wants to dream of her future husband, she should recite this prayer before going to bed:

Sweet St. Lucy, let me know
whose cloth I shall lay,
whose bed I shall make, whose child I shall bear, whose
darling I shall be, whose arms I shall lie in.

St. Thomas (December 20)

To dream of your future husband with the assistance of St. Thomas, try this technique:

Tonight, get an onion, cut it in half, and stick a pin in the center of it. Stick eight more pins around the first circle. Then recite the following:

Good St. Thomas, do me right
And let my true love come tonight,
That I may see him in the face
And in my arms may him embrace.

Put the onion under your pillow when you go to sleep, and you will see your future husband. Using a sweet onion may help alleviate the odor.

St. Anthony (January 17)

St. Anthony, who found the lost herd of sheep in the Italian city of
Padua, is the patron saint of lost articles. He was a kind man, and
many believe that he is the one to go to if you have lost something.
Ask St. Anthony to help you find a long-lost love.

Recite this twist on a St. Anthony prayer:

Tony, Tony, look around,
My love is lost and must be found.
If you bring him back to me,
I will be grateful eternally!

St. Dwynwen (January 25)

As the Welsh legend goes, after having a fight with her boyfriend, St. Dwynwen became a nun in order to never marry. Some believe that by saying her name on her day, true lovers will achieve their heart's desire or recover from heartache.

Here is a little prayer you can use any day to find a lover:

St. Dwynwen,
We beseech thee, comfort lovers whose vision is unclear.
Send mending to those with love lost. Protect our
companions.
In your name we seek to do the same
In your name, we choose love first.

St. Valentine (February 14)

St. Valentine is the saint most tied to love. Most single people dread his day because it is drenched in twosomeness. Don't worry; good St. Valentine can help you find your perfect mate to spend V-Day with next year.

Prayer to find a lover:

Blessed St. Valentine, I come to you with a heart full of love, yearning to share its fullness with another. Help me find this person to share my life, which I pledge to fill with understanding, courtesy, fidelity, and temperance. Let the law of kindness rule my life and govern all I say and do. Be with me on my search, Blessed Valentine, and guide my way to one who will care for me as I will care for my life's partner.

St. Drago (April 16)

St. Drago is the patron saint for ugly people. Apparently, he was very ugly but loved by many nonetheless. Even if you're pretty, wouldn't you love to have someone who loves you for your inner beauty? Ask St. Drago to help you find someone, using this prayer:

Drago, you were loved
Despite your lack of external beauty.
You had faith and courage.
Please intercede on my behalf,
Help me find a love honest and true.

St. Anne (July 26)

Anne was the mother of Mary. Many women pray to her and ask for help in the love department. If you really want to get him with St. Anne's help, try this novena (a prayer that is said for nine consecutive days):

> *Dear St. Anne*
> *Send me a man*
> *As quick as you can.*

See what happens on day ten.

St. Catherine (November 25)

St. Catherine is the patron saint of so-called old maids or spinsters—such archaic terms! Many single women have asked her for help in seeking a lover. Try this prayer and hope for the best:

Sweet St. Catherine, send me a husband,
A good one, I pray,
But any one better than none.
Oh, St. Catherine, lend me thine aid,
That I may not die an old maid.

São Gonçalo (June 7)

São Gonçalo is the patron saint of lovers in Portugal. The Portuguese even have a festival to celebrate his day and his matchmaking abilities. In the town of Amarante, unmarried men and women exchange penis-shaped cakes to express their affection for each other. Why not try making some penis-shaped cakes and pass them out to friends? It may not bring true love, but what a conversation piece! (No pun intended.)

St. John (June 24)

St. John the Baptist is one of the most important figures in Christianity. He was a fisherman who spent his days on the ocean, prophesying of things to come.

Here's a Polish tradition that involves water and a little foreshadowing. Send a wreath with a candle down a river or stream, or out on the ocean. If it floats away, you will marry. If a man catches your wreath, it is said that he is destined to marry you.

St. John's Day is midsummer, and many traditions associated with saints tie in with pagan traditions that fell at the same time. Here is a tradition associated with St. John that probably has ties to another belief. Either way, it should help bring some clarity to your love life, so give it a whirl. Rise at dawn on St. John's Day and break an egg into a glass half-filled with water. Leave it there until the sun sets. By sunset, the mixture may have a pungent odor, but according to folklore, you will be able to see the face of your future lover in it.

St. Simon and St. Jude (October 28)

On St. Simon and St. Jude's Day, you can divine your future husband by peeling an apple in one long strip. Then, take the peel in your right hand, spin around three times, and say:

Saints Simon and Jude, on you I intrude,
By this paring I hold to discover
Without any delay, to tell me this day
The first letter of my own true lover.

Then drop the peel over your left shoulder, and the first initial of the man's surname will appear. According to tradition, if the peel breaks into pieces, you will never marry. You might want to practice this one before reciting the prayer!

St. Isidore (April 4)

St. Isidore was a great scholar and communicator. He wrote the famous *Etymologies*, which is akin to an encyclopedia of all the knowledge of his day. Although it was written in the early seventh century, this work is similar in structure to a modern database, and because of this, Isidore has been named the patron saint of the Internet.

St. Isidore was also famous for helping those in need. Log on to an online dating service and ask St. Isidore to help you find Mr. Right. Choose a sexy picture and give yourself a hot code name like "sassylassie."

St. Barbara (December 4)

Barbara was a beauty. Her overprotective father locked her in a tower with two windows to keep her "safe" from suitors. When Barbara's father was away, she had a third window installed in the tower against her father's will. Upon his return, he had her sentenced to death for her rebellious act—tough dad! During her stay in the tower, a branch of a cherry tree got trapped in the door. The branch bloomed after her death, revealing her sanctity, and leading to the following tradition.

A young unattached girl cuts branches from a fruit tree and puts them into a vase. If they begin to blossom before Christmas Eve, it means she is certain to get married in the next year.

Seasons and Celebrations

We mark our time with seasons: spring—a time of birth and regrowth, summer—long days and fun-filled nights, fall—a time for gathering, winter—the end of the year and a time to reflect on what's important.

It's funny how our temperament often reflects the season of the year. One thing for sure, any time of the year is a good time to seek love. For centuries, women have known this is true, and these seasonal love strategies are best used during certain times of the year. Make a love wreath in the spring, dance in the summer, walk by candlelight in the fall, and enjoy time with new friends in the winter. Get caught up in celebrations and swept off your feet by someone new!

Passion Fruit Day

(February 1)

This fragrant golden fruit is native to Brazil and has a sweet-tart taste. It was given its name by the Spanish missionaries. They thought the fruit and the plant had a particularly close resemblance to the crown of thorns associated with the crucifixion. But the juicy passion fruit also has some love powers in February, the month associated with love. If you kiss a passion fruit today, your love fantasies will come true.

Eve of St. Valentine's Day (February 13)

St. Valentine's Day at mid-February is the day set aside for lovers to express their unending love for one another. However, the eve of St. Valentine's Day has been marked for eligible women to learn who their future love will be. From Great Britain to Belarus, many have tested this divination. Try it this year and have a Valentine next year.

To see your dearly beloved in a dream, take five bay leaves and tie them to your pillow. Make sure one of the leaves is set in the center of your pillow. The other four should be fastened to the corners. You will dream of your soul mate all night long.

St. Valentine's Day (February 14)

Hearts, Cupids, bows and arrows, chocolates, and love letters are all associated with this day. Everyone, from pagans to Christians, claims this holiday as their own. The one constant they share is that this day, above all others, is a day for love. Everything about today exudes love; even some birds choose their mates on this day.

Here's a way to find your lover:

Let a single woman go out of her own door very early in the morning, and if the first person she meets be a woman, she will not be married that year; if she meets a man, she will be married within three months.

Before you go out, plan your route with men in mind!

Then, one month to the day after Valentine's Day, comes White Day, March 14. In Japan on this day the men who received gifts of chocolate on Valentine's Day must return the favor. Chocolates packaged in white boxes are priced higher on this day than a month earlier. White Day was established in 1980, and some think that it's just a chocolate maker's conspiracy.

We say you should remember those fellows you bestowed your affection on, and take the chocolate with a smile.

Lupercalia Festival
(February 15)

Some people believe Lupercalia is the true origin of St. Valentine's Day. This annual spring celebration and uniquely Roman festival was celebrated with a lover lottery. Names of single young women were put into a box and were drawn out by men. The new couple was then required to accept each other as their love for the duration of the festival. If they were lucky, sometimes it would last a lifetime.

Have a singles party. Invite your single friends and have them each bring an unattached friend of the opposite sex. Put the guys' names in a box and have the women draw a partner. See if your lottery produces a winning match for you.

Ladies' Day/Bachelors' Day (February 29)

The earth actually takes longer than 365 days to complete its trip around the sun. Five hours forty-eight minutes and forty-five seconds longer. To accommodate this, an extra day is added to the Gregorian calendar in February every four years. The year in which it occurs is called leap year—probably because the English courts did not always recognize February 29, and that date was often "leaped over" in records.

There's an old tradition that women could propose marriage to men during leap year. The men had to pay a forfeit fine if they refused. February 29 is often referred to as Ladies' Day or Bachelors' Day.

Go for it today! We're not saying propose to a complete stranger, but by simply introducing yourself, you could use this anniversary to propose in four years.

Sadie Hawkins Day
(November 9)

If we can jump ahead to November for a moment, let us mention Sadie Hawkins Day, when women have the same privilege. "Ladies, grab yer partners," said Alfred Gerald Caplin (a.k.a. Al Capp), who first invented Sadie Hawkins Day in his syndicated comic strip *Li'l Abner*. He conjured up the idea in 1938, when he announced November 9 as an occasion when single women in the mythical town of Dogpatch could pursue eligible bachelors, who were in turn obliged to marry them. Communities have since taken it upon themselves to celebrate November 9 with dances and other ceremonies. Though men aren't obliged to marry their female suitors, they are expected to at least be a courteous date.

Shouting in a Rain Barrel

On the first day of spring, try shouting at the top of your lungs into a rain barrel at the corner of your house. If you hear an echo, you will marry the next unmarried man who comes your way.

Keep your ears open. Also, if you hear a dove coo, the next person of the opposite sex that you meet will be your mate.

Tax Day
(April 15)

There is an old saying: "There are only two things for certain in life—death and taxes." Today, pay the taxes. Perhaps the one thing more draining in life than finding a date is filling out all those tax forms and watching your money go to some guy named Sam, and you don't even get a kiss! Here's an idea that may make the whole process a little more entertaining.

Pick a peak time and go to your local post office. There you will find plenty of single men filing their taxes. If you want to find a wealthy one, try going to a post office in a glitzy neighborhood. You know, 90210.

Earth Day
(April 22)

In hopes of bringing about some awareness of the environment, Senator Gaylord Nelson initiated the first Earth Day in 1970 on college campuses nationwide. This grassroots celebration has become a national festivity celebrated annually with pride.

Go to an Earth Day festival and find yourself a Birk-wearing, hemp-weaving, patchouli-smelling, granola hottie. If sparks fly, plant an orange tree together; this is the tree of love and marriage.

Semik Festival

This Russian festival usually takes place on the seventh Thursday after Easter. Young women go into the forest to gather flowers. They make them into wreaths and throw them into the stream. If they float, the women will be married in a year. Make a floral wreath; throw it into a river, stream, ocean, or even your bathtub. If it floats. . . .

April 29

May Day is the official celebration of Summer. A pre-pre-May Day tradition will reveal a clue to finding your mate in a most peculiar way.

On the evening of April 29, spread a handkerchief on the lawn under a tree, and the next morning you will find on the handkerchief the initial of your future mate.

May Eve

(April 30)

This is the time of year when there are many rituals to help you find clues about your future lover. Many of them reveal the initials of his name, including this one.

On the last day of April, wash a handkerchief and hang it that night on a stalk of corn, or spread it over growing wheat in the field, or drape it over a rosebush in the garden. The morning sun of May will dry it, and the initials of the man you are to marry will appear in the wrinkles of the handkerchief.

May Day
(May 1)

May Day is the time of milk and honey. Also called Beltane by the Celts, it is the last of the three seasons of fertility. It is when the flowers bloom and declare victory over the winter snow. Dormant trees and seeds awaken and sprout new leaves and bloom. Spring has arrived; it's a great time to fall in love!

Rise before dawn on May 1 and wash your face with field dew. It will bring youth or love anew.

Midsummer Games

Midsummer is usually celebrated in late June. The pagan festivities celebrated longer days and a break from the taxing work routines—more time for romance and courting. It was also a time of mysticism and aligning with the spirits. William Shakespeare expressed the same themes in his play *A Midsummer Night's Dream*, in which love and magic fill the night.

Up for a late-night snack? In seventeenth-century England, it was customary for girls to hold a "dumb supper" or "silent supper" on Midsummer's Eve. The late meal was to be prepared in total darkness, without one word spoken between the participants. Everything was placed backwards, including the silverware, china, even the chairs at the table. Servers walked backwards from the kitchen and courses were eaten in reverse order. Then, still in complete silence and darkness, the girls would wait until the clock struck midnight. At that time, each would see before her the ghostly form of her future husband.

If all that seems too complicated, here's another midsummer tale: tear a fresh fig leaf, and if the break heals before morning, you will find your true love.

Flour Power

Try this midsummer ritual: Set a plate of flour under a rosemary bush. The next morning you will see the initials of your future husband traced in the flour.

✳ Where to find it ✳

You can pick up a small rosemary bush at your local farmer's market or nursery.

It's Not Just for Breakfast Anymore

This Bulgarian midsummer ritual tells young women their fortunes.

Drop a ring tied with a red thread and ivy into a bowl of water with oats and barley, and leave them overnight. Dance around the bowl and have your fortune told. If you don't have a Bulgarian Gypsy nearby, go to your local fortuneteller with bowl in hand.

Michaelmas
(September 28 and October 10)

Autumn—a perfect time to "fall" in love. If you're not sure which guy to pick, try picking some crab apples. The old English custom of "Crabbing for Husbands" had girls collect crab apples on September 28 and arrange them to form the initials of their boyfriends or love interests. Then they would see which ones lasted the longest through October 10, or Old Michaelmas Day; these would be the prospective suitors. Try this to see who your man is.

Fontinalia
(October 13)

Today is a day to celebrate the Camenae, water spirits who live in freshwater springs, rivers, and the sacred spring at Porta Capena near Rome. This old Roman festival celebrates them and the luck they award the deserving.

On this day, good luck wreaths are tossed into wells as a devotion to the spirit. Make a good luck wreath with rosemary, all the while thinking about your love wishes. Hide a penny in the wreath and toss it into a well or fountain with a wish to the water spirits.

Halloween
(October 31)

Name an apple for your love interest and suspend it from a string on Halloween. If you can bite into it on the first try, you are loved by that person.

Another time-honored tradition on this frightful night is bobbing for apples. Apples would have names cut into them and then get submerged in a tub of water. Then people would bob for the apples and try to secure one with their teeth. Once a woman secured an apple, she would read the name to reveal who her future husband would be.

All Souls' Day
(November 2)

It is said that if you visit a garden on the night of All Souls, you will see your future spouse. Go by candlelight and, with your eyes closed, pick the first cabbage you touch. The shape of the cabbage will be the likeness of your guy. If there is soil on the roots, he will be a rich one, and if the stem is sweet so will your life be with your love.

Thanksgiving Wishbone

Save the Thanksgiving wishbone! Make it work for you twice:
First, make a wish while breaking the wishbone with a friend.
Then, put your portion over the door. You will marry the first
single man who enters.

St. Andrew's Eve (November 29)

In Polish tradition, St. Andrew's Eve is a perfect night to play games that will predict who your mate will be. Here is one of the more popular games. Write down the names of various men you have your eye on and paste each one in a walnut shell. Make one shell with your name in it. Put them all in a tub of water and gently rock the tub. As the water settles, watch—the name that floats closest to yours is the name of the guy you will couple with.

Paper Wishes (December 11)

Winter is for wishing. On the evening of December 11, take twelve pieces of paper and write eleven random men's names on them, one on each, leaving one piece blank. Roll them up and put them in a box. Starting on December 12, take one name out of the box each day and burn it without looking at it. On December 24, read the remaining name—the name of your future partner. (Hopefully, it's not the blank piece of paper.)

December Yule Log
(December 22)

During this holiday season, get together with your single girlfriends for a night of cocktails and Yuletide prophecy. Traditionally in Europe the lighting of the Yule log was a ceremonious event. Choose a log to go into the fire. Have each woman tie a different colored string around it. Put it in the fire. The first string to burn through signifies who will be the first one to be wed.

Christmas Day (December 25)

Who would have thought that cleaning up the Christmas table could give you a key to finding love?

This year, collect all the crumbs from the dinner table and run outside with them. Hold them in your hand until you hear somebody shouting a man's name. That is the name of your future husband.

And keep your Christmas tree meaningful by making it a wishing tree. Try this tradition that was popular among many in the 1920s: Hang envelopes with good thoughts on the tree with ribbon.

✦ Today's Twist ✦

Invite your single friends over, enclose a love prophecy in each envelope, and have each friend select a prophecy for the New Year.

Christmas Wishbone

If you didn't like the results of the Thanksgiving wishbone, try again! Hang a wishbone over the door between Christmas and New Year's. The first unattached guy who passes through the door will be your future husband. Maybe you should try this at work, in order to increase the pool of possible men.

Twelfth Night
(January 5)

Also known as the Eve of the Epiphany, Twelfth Night marks the arrival of the three kings at the manger. It is one of the oldest Christian feasts, celebrated since the second century. In Romania, young unwed women try this trick today. Go to bed without eating. It will bring you luck in finding a handsome and hardworking man. Don't mistake this for a new diet, but with all that food over the holidays, skipping dinner couldn't hurt the waistline.

Epiphany
(January 6)

A Romanian Ephiphany tradition for love involves a little foliage and takes advantage of the winter chill. In the evening, put sweet basil on the fence of your house. In the morning, if the branch is covered with white frost you will have a rich husband, and if the branch is not covered in white frost, you will have a poor husband.

You might want to throw in a little prayer for a cold spell if you live in the warmer climates. It couldn't hurt!

New Year's Eve
(December 31)

Whether you have found a mate or not this year, here's an old custom that is sure to predict if you will hear wedding bells in the coming year. Find an old shoe, preferably with long laces. Throw it up into the branches of a willow tree. If the shoe drops to the ground, you will have to wait another year. But if the shoe gets caught in the leaves and branches, you are sure to walk down the aisle in the next 365 days.

Bonza Bottler Day

Here's a celebration for all seasons. Any day on which the day and the month share the same number—January 1 (1/1), February 2 (2/2), etc.—is called Bonza Bottler day. It is really just an excuse to celebrate.

Any day when the numbers are aligned would be a great day to see a numerologist. Find out what your numbers say about you, and when romance is going to come your way.

Modern Twist

What's old is new again! Just as with fashion, we can look to what was once popular and make it hip for today. Love is never out of fashion; in fact, there is potential for love everywhere. Hold your head up, stride out your front door, and try something new. Pick up a hobby, a sport, an opportunity to volunteer, or something else that's completely new. Or create your own opportunities by hosting a new kind of singles event. Once in a while, people can fall into a rut and all they need is a little shake-up.

Be adventurous! Be brave! Just get out there!

Blue for Boys

When Count Fieschi of Lavagna in Genoa, Italy, threw a wedding party in 1240, it was a celebration. The centerpiece alone was a thirty-foot cake called the Torta dei Fieschi, which was shared with the entire town. In remembrance of his generosity, the celebration continues yearly. People dress in costumes and parade through the town square, where they pin to their clothes a piece of paper on which a word is written. Blue for men, white for women. When they find someone wearing the same word, the couple is given a piece of cake.

Have a singles bash! Make sure your guest list is an equal number of males and females. Brainstorm with your friends as to what new prospects you each can invite for each other. In advance, prepare enough blue and white pieces of paper with matching words, so that all guests will have one to wear upon their arrival. Later that night, announce, "It is time to find your match and share a slice of decadence!"

Saucy Delight

Fondue comes from the mountain people in Switzerland. They created this delight in the cold months, when food was scarce and they had to use what was available for nourishment. There was plenty of cheese. Fondue became popular again in the 1970s. Those '70s swingers knew how to throw a party! Go retro and have a fondue party or go to a fondue bar. Get that sensual, ooey-gooey cheesy delight all over yourself, and have someone help you clean up the mess—napkins optional.

Ask Away!

The Asking Festival takes place among the Inuit Eskimos in Alaska yearly. Everyone from the village gathers, and each man makes a request from a woman in the village. She is then required to deliver. In return, she is allowed to request something back from the asker. Have a white elephant party. Invite your single girl and guy friends. Keeping love as the theme, have them bring personal items they are willing to part with and let the asking begin!

Altair and Vega

The Japanese celebration called The Star Festival honors two separated lovers. Altair, a cow herder, fell in love with Vega, a weaver. When they married, their love for each other was so strong that they neglected their professions and spent every moment with each other. This behavior got them in trouble, and they were forced to live on opposite sides of the Milky Way. But once a year, on the seventh day of the seventh month, they are joined with the help of the celestial magpies who build a bridge across the Milky Way. In Japan this is celebrated by hanging colorful strips of paper on bamboo branches.

Wear a colorful outfit and try this fun practice. It is said that if you tie a blue satin ribbon around your ankle, you will be kissed by the day's end. Turn an old superstition into a fashion statement, cross your celestial bridge, and pucker up.

Maybe You Can
Get a Man with a Gun

Annie Oakley was famed for her shooting skills and was known as "little sure shot." Annie didn't hold back when she wanted a man, which was lucky for her husband Frank Butler, the love of her life. Not only could she outshoot him, she made her romantic intentions known. Their love affair was so deep and united that he died seven days after she did. Find the Annie Oakley spirit in you today and go to your local shooting range. See if you can't outshoot that cute cowboy next to you.

Decorating for Love

Feng Shui or "wind, water" is symbolically where we live between heaven and earth. There is an invisible energy called *chi* that flows throughout this space. The art of Feng Shui is finding that energy and working with it to gain a balance (yin and yang). The arrangement of the house and garden helps the chi work to your advantage, bringing you success, health, wealth, happiness, and love.

Have you Feng Shui'd your environment yet? The right rear corner of your room (from the entry door) is the most optimal corner for love. Here are some ideas to give that corner a little help. Try decorating the corner with love tokens such as hearts, red or pink candles, and pictures of love scenes. Maybe you can drape a romantic scarf over a table or hang some love beads in the corner. Channel the love energy from that corner every day and use it to help you find your true love.

Arresting Developments

Looking for a guy in uniform? How about your local police officer? They are bold, they are brave, and they look so good in blue. Support your local department by attending the annual Policemen's Ball. See if your neighborhood law enforcer can teach you a few tricks with his handcuffs! Oh, this could be a 911 emergency....

Is It Hot in Here?

Who could forget to thank her local firefighters for all their hard work? These guys spend countless hours at the fire station. They cook, they clean, and they keep themselves in shape. What more could a woman ask for? Try out their delicious delights at the next pancake breakfast or chili cookoff. Have him set your heart aflame. Don't worry—he knows fire safety.

Get Back to Nature

Remember summer camp and the cute boy with the fisherman's hat? You pined over him all week. Well, time to go camping as a grownup and make your move on the cute guy this time. Plan a trip with your single girlfriends to go water rafting or hiking with any club or organization that caters to singles and offers a good time.

Heart on a String

Get yourself a colorful kite and go fly it at your local park or beach. Bask in the sun and soak up the energy of the wind. See if you can create some electricity of your own. Find a guy who can help you set your kite aflight. If you are really brave, you might want to try hang gliding with a sexy instructor who can help strap you in and set your love life soaring.

Horsin' Around

Who didn't want a pony as a little girl? And who doesn't think cowboys are sexy? Head to the nearest stable and go on a trail ride—maybe your trail leader will be the man of your dreams. Ride 'em, cowgirl!

Come Back to Me

The yo-yo is the oldest toy in history, next to the doll. Yo-yo means "come back" in Pilipino, and people have been playing with yo-yos "around the world" for centuries.

Do you remember the yo-yo game? Practice a bit before you start this one, because you want to get it right this time. Let the yo-yo unravel to the end of the string and climb back up again. Count the number of times you complete this cycle without interruption. The letter of the alphabet that corresponds to that number is the first initial of the name of the man you are destined to meet.

Hit the Pavement

Sign up for a local 5K or 10K run. If you are really fit, go for a marathon. Make training fun and join a training team. This is a great way to build a race support network and meet lots of interesting guys—while at the same time finding out if they can keep up with you. Don't play *too* hard to get.

Sun Salutations

Take a yoga class. Not only will it help center your heart and body, but there are lots of limber guys to stretch and take deep cleansing breaths with. The breath of fire is even sexier than it sounds.

From Petals to Pedals

Get yourself into one of those cute little bike outfits and ride at the beach, in the mountains, or around town. Maybe join a training team. Keep your eyes out for any good-looking bikers along the way. There's nothing like scoping out prospective mates while getting some fresh air and burning some calories.

Go Where the Swingers Are

How can so many people (especially men!) be fanatic about a game with a little ball and a stick? Golf has become one of America's hottest pastimes and fastest growing sports. The golf course is one of the places where women are outnumbered by men. Take a golf lesson or go to the driving range. You should have plenty of men to choose from there. Stand near a cute guy and ask for his opinion on your swing.

Live Bait

Everything about fishing is for the boys, from buying worms to filleting your catch, and everything in between. Be where the guys are—go on a fishing expedition. You are certain to hook a hottie on this trip. Lure him in!

Joy Stick

Women are the fastest growing group of gamers right now. If you think it's only for kids, you're wrong. For every gamer under the age of eighteen, there are two who are over eighteen. Head on down to your local video game store or cybercafe and find out what's in the top ten. The guy-to-girl ratio there is also strongly in your favor. A boyishly handsome gamer will have a very cozy couch to cuddle up on together.

Power Play

Hockey is another sport dominated by men—some without teeth. The energy around a hockey game is exhilarating, and the parties afterwards are known to be lots of fun. Go to a hockey game, either pro or a local league. Make a power play of your own.

To the Races!

Head to the racetrack. Next to baseball, horse racing is the most attended sport in America. Whether you spring for the VIP seats or go general admission, place your bet on love. Mingle in the crowd and pick your favorites . . . horses and guys alike. Racing is known as the "sport of kings," so keep your eyes open for your prince.

Play Ball!

"Take me out to the ball game. . . ." Pick a team and root them on! At the ballpark you will see some cuties running bases and have the opportunity to bond with some of your handsome fellow fans. Local parks have leagues. Join a co-ed team or pick a guys' team and become their cheerleader. Hey batter, batter!

Love: 40

How can you not like a game where there's a score called Love?
Take a class from some handsome tennis pro. Join a tennis club or
hang out at your local tennis courts and find yourself a partner to
"play" with—nudge, nudge, wink, wink!

The Kiss, by Rodin

Paintings, sculpture, photography? Impressionist, modern, avant-garde? Whatever style of art you prefer, take a tour at your local art museum. Find out what inspired the artists to create their masterpieces. Attend the gallery talks, grab a handsome docent for a private tour. Take an art class and see what develops. Discover the muse within yourself and free her!

Feast!

Try a new restaurant. Get dressed up and take yourself out to
dinner. Stop in the bar for a drink first. Perhaps there is another
solo diner looking for some company. If he's really cute, maybe you
can share dessert.

Matchmaker, Matchmaker

The Jewish matchmaking festival was meant to set up young Jewish bachelors with their future brides. The ladies would dress in white and dance through the vineyards. Surely there were a few yentas on hand to help out. And who knows love better than a yenta? Go get yourself to a modern-day yenta and have her find you the perfect match.

✴ Today's twist ✴

Try an online search to find a modern-day matchmaker.

Look for the Signs

In the past, the advice of psychics and fortunetellers was sought in secret. Today they have TV shows and 1-800 numbers. Get a reading from a tarot card reader, numerologist, or astrologer. Ask them about your future love. Sometimes there are signs of love all around us that we need a little help seeing.

Be Late, Find Love.

The question is: "What would be different if you missed your morning train or bus today?" You usually see the same faces on your morning commute. Who would you see and meet if you went to work ten minutes later? Tell your boss you did it for love. She'll understand.

Love Ballot

In 1920, women's empowerment took a huge leap forward when women were granted the right to vote. Since then, women have assumed many powerful roles in politics, including congresswomen, governors, and senators.

Empower yourself by getting out there and joining a political campaign. Look for some hot politico that you can share your beliefs with. Remember, vote for love!

Road Trip!

Hit the highway. Take a road trip of your own. Make it a day trip
to a place you have never been. Think about going somewhere
that you've heard is full of eligible bachelors. Coast through town
on foot and rub elbows with the local prospects.

The Core of the Matter

Oh true love, where can he be? Here, there, just about anywhere. Being the adventurous woman that you are, it's time to go find him!

Try this old superstition and use modern technology (like a train or plane) to get you there. Flick an apple seed onto a map. Where it lands will indicate where you will find true love. Hit the road—Johnny Appleseed is waiting!

Lady Godiva

A surefire way to get the attention of many is to ride naked through your town. However, you may end up in jail, and that's no place to meet Mr. Right. Go to a nude beach instead and shed your clothes and inhibitions!

Marilyn

She was born Norma Jean Baker, but was known to the world as
Marilyn Monroe. This international sex goddess knew what to
do with what she had. She married a baseball star and a famous
playwright, and had an affair with a president. By using both her
beauty and her wits, she could have any man she wanted. As a
tribute to Marilyn, dress up in your sexiest outfit and feel what
it's like to be a sex symbol. If you are truly brave, go sing "Happy
Birthday, Mr. President" at a karaoke bar.

Volunteer for Love

Not the sex symbol type? Take your inspiration from Maid Marian, her love for Robin Hood, and their tradition of giving to the poor. Go to your local soup kitchen and help pass out a meal, or help with preparations. Perhaps you will find your modern-day Robin Hood standing next to you.

Or honor Florence Nightingale by volunteering at your local Red Cross this week. Good for your conscience, good for your heart—and you never know who will walk in the door to donate, or who will be working with you, shoulder to shoulder.

Sneak a Kiss

In 1984, the world's longest kiss was recorded at 17 days, 10.5 hours. How romantic! Why not try to set your own record. Or at least try to beat your personal best today.

Kissing is so much fun! But do we kiss enough? And is there a right way to kiss? Eyes open or closed, wet lips or dry, tongue or not. Perhaps there really is an art to this activity. Figure it all out and to be sneaky about it (if that is possible). Go up to a guy you have your eye on and plant one on him. You decide the mechanics of it. Smooch away.

Friends and Lovers

A friend is someone you can go to in time of need, a pal you can share your secrets with, laugh with, cry with, and celebrate life with. Wow, wouldn't someone like that make a great partner too? Some believe the best lovers are your best friends. Take a second look at your best male friends. Maybe one of them could be the one?

Be Prepared

Love is lurking around every corner and often comes when you are least expecting it. Have fun while using these suggestions. The road to love is full of adventures, but even race car drivers take precautions, so be smart with your heart.

Remember, the love you are looking for is out there. Be daring, be safe, and be ready!

To Our Readers